THE HUNT FOR PLANET NINE

Contents

Can you trust your senses?	2
1 We don't know … how many planets there are!	4
2 We don't know … how big our solar system is!	12
3 We don't know … how the planets got their strange features!	22
4 We don't know … how the Sun works!	34
Space detectives	42
Glossary	44
Index	45
An astronaut's diary	46

Written by Isabel Thomas
Illustrated by Shane Tolentino

Collins

Can you trust your senses?

Look at the sky on a clear night. What can you see and feel?

Earth feels completely still. Space looks empty, apart from the Moon and tiny, twinkling stars.

But scientists know that we can't always trust our senses. Our planet is always moving. It zooms around the Sun once every year. It spins once every day.

Earth is not alone. Billions of other objects also zoom around the Sun. They include planets, moons and smaller chunks of rock, metal and ice.

Everything that travels around (or **orbits**) the Sun is part of our **solar system**.

Scientists have learnt lots about our solar system. The things they know already fill hundreds of books. But they are more interested in what we *don't* know. Some of those things might surprise you!

1 We don't know ... how many planets there are!

Earth is a planet. Planets are huge. You might think they would be easy to count.

But over the last 250 years, the number has changed many times. Today, we count eight planets.

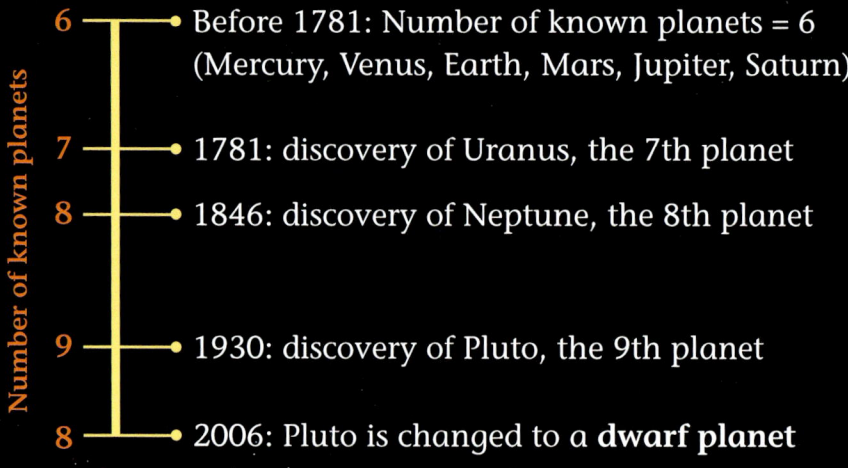

- Before 1781: Number of known planets = 6 (Mercury, Venus, Earth, Mars, Jupiter, Saturn)
- 1781: discovery of Uranus, the 7th planet
- 1846: discovery of Neptune, the 8th planet
- 1930: discovery of Pluto, the 9th planet
- 2006: Pluto is changed to a **dwarf planet**

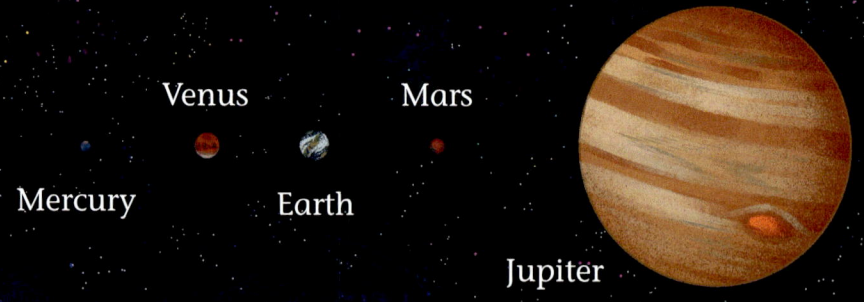

Features of a planet
- ✔ Spherical (ball-shaped)
- ✔ Orbits the Sun and nothing else
- ✔ Doesn't share its orbit

Is Pluto a planet?

For a long time, people called Pluto the ninth planet. It is spherical and it orbits the Sun. However, Pluto shares its orbit with Charon, a moon almost half its size! So Pluto has been renamed a dwarf planet.

Pluto   Charon

Saturn   Uranus   Neptune

Scientists still think that a ninth planet may be lurking at the edge of our solar system. No one has seen Planet Nine, but scientists have found clues that it might be there.

The clues come from small, icy chunks found far from the Sun. Scientists have noticed a wobble in the orbit that these objects take around the Sun.

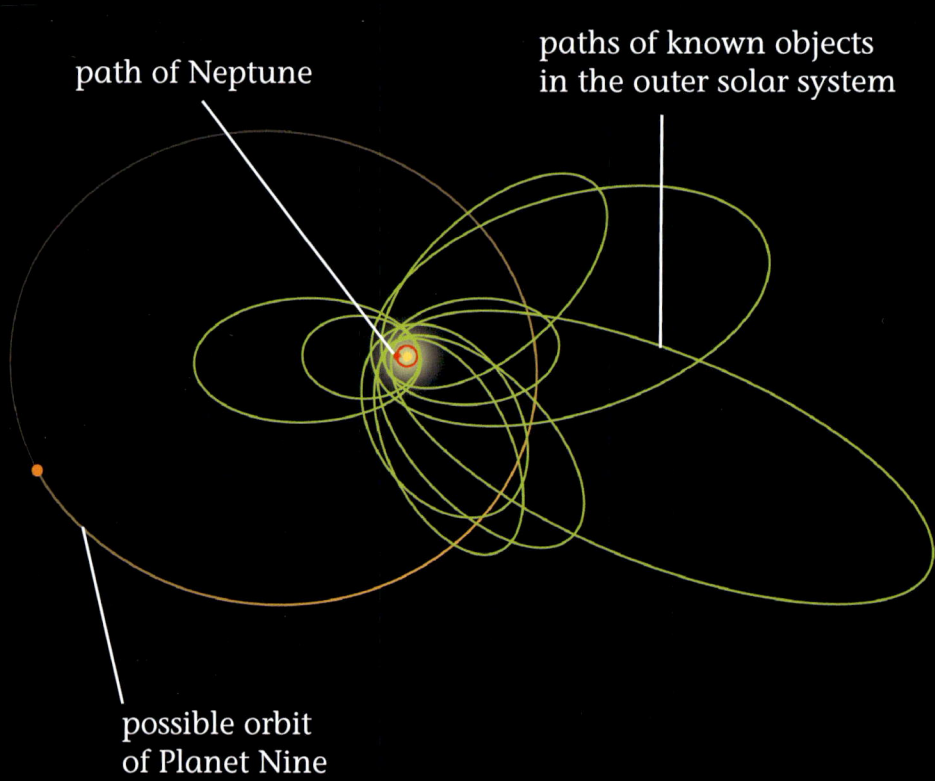

path of Neptune

paths of known objects in the outer solar system

possible orbit of Planet Nine

It is like something is tugging on them. This could be the **gravity** of a much larger object – Planet Nine.

Scientists have even predicted what Planet Nine is like.

cold and icy

500 times further from the Sun than Earth

bigger than Earth but smaller than Neptune

one year lasts for 10,000 Earth years

Scientists are using powerful **telescopes** to search for Planet Nine.

The Rubin Observatory will help with the search. It has a good view of space from the top of a mountain in South America.

This is not the first time scientists have hunted for a planet. Neptune and Pluto were both predicted to exist before they were found.

Spotting a giant planet might sound easy.
But our solar system is enormous, and its objects are constantly moving. It is like trying to find a single fish hiding somewhere in Earth's oceans.

New objects are spotted in our solar system every year. In 2023, scientists spotted moons of Uranus and Neptune that they had never noticed before.

DISCOVERY OF THE PLANET PLUTO

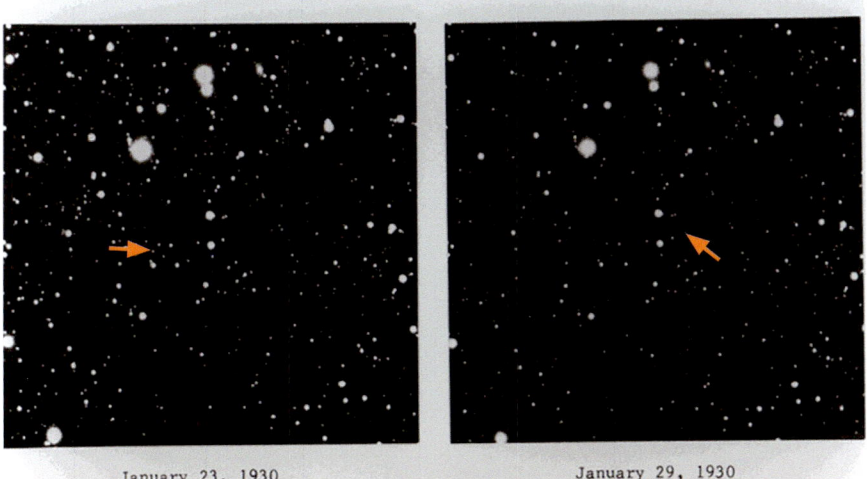

January 23, 1930   January 29, 1930

It is difficult, but possible. These photographs were used to discover Pluto. After 7,000 hours of comparing photographs, a scientist noticed that one small dot had moved. The dot is Pluto, on its way around the Sun!

Of course, Planet Nine might not exist. Some scientists have come up with different ideas to explain the wonky paths of the small, icy chunks:

a tiny **black hole**

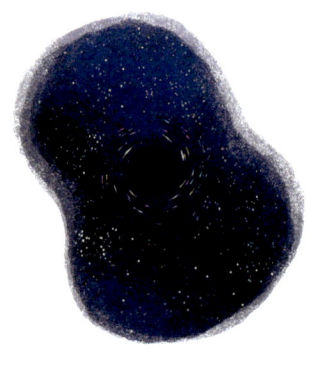

an invisible dust cloud

a planet from a different solar system

a mistake in their calculations

What do you think? Could Planet Nine be real?

Naming Planet Nine

If someone does spot Planet Nine, they will get to choose its proper name. Most planets are named after Roman and Greek gods and goddesses. These are some names that have not been used yet. Which one would you pick?

Terminus

Fons

Vulcan   Salus

Novensides   Flora   Pales

Lucina   Bacchus

Genius

2 We don't know ... how big our solar system is!

The Sun lies at the centre of our solar system.

The Sun is the largest, brightest object in our solar system. So, it's easy to see where the solar system starts.

However, no one knows where the solar system ends.

Everything that orbits the Sun is part of our solar system. But most of these objects are impossible to see.

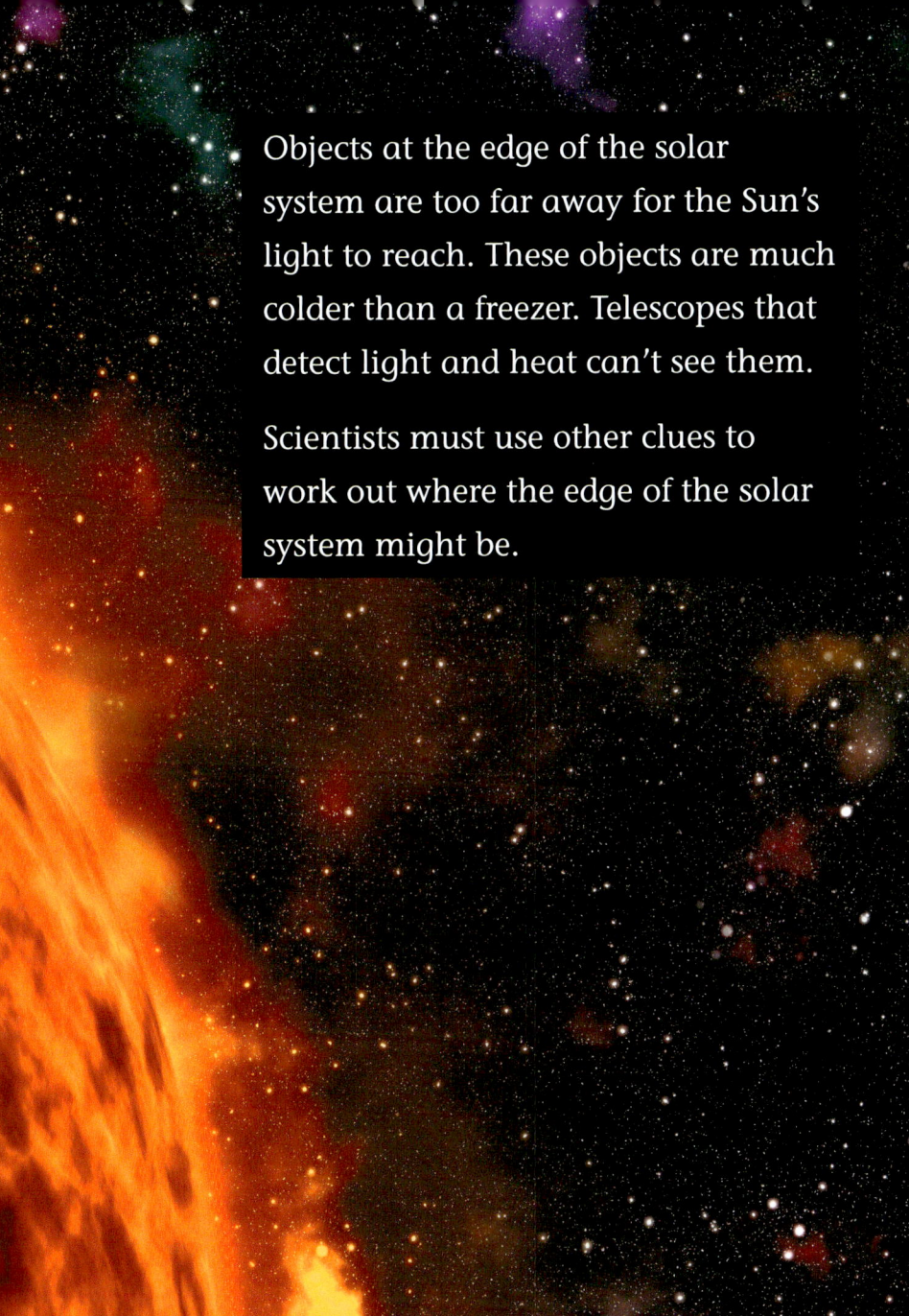

Objects at the edge of the solar system are too far away for the Sun's light to reach. These objects are much colder than a freezer. Telescopes that detect light and heat can't see them.

Scientists must use other clues to work out where the edge of the solar system might be.

Of all the objects spotted in the solar system so far, Sedna is one of the furthest from the Sun.

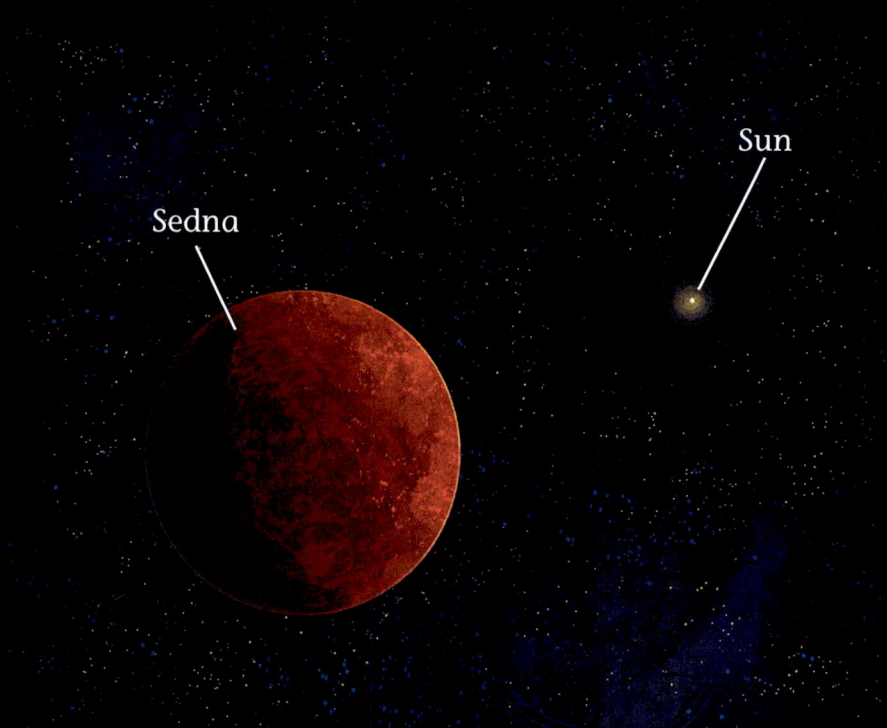

Sedna is a dwarf planet, a little smaller than Pluto. It is named after the Inuit goddess of the ocean.

When Sedna was first spotted in 2003, it was the most distant object ever seen in our solar system. It was almost 90 times further from the Sun than Earth is. But scientists believe the solar system is even bigger than this.

They think that the inner solar system – the part with all the planets and dwarf planets – is surrounded by a giant cloud of small, icy objects. Each one slowly orbits the Sun in frozen darkness.

Oort Cloud

This cloud is called the Oort Cloud. It is named after one of the scientists that came up with the idea.

No one has ever seen an object in the Oort Cloud. So why are scientists so sure it exists?

The best **evidence** for the Oort Cloud comes from something that we *can* see:

Comets are rock-hard balls of ice the size of cities. We can only see them when they are near the Sun.

But scientists think they come from the darkest, coldest part of the solar system: the Oort Cloud.

The story of a comet

Imagine this: You are an icy snowball so far away that the Sun looks like a tiny speck, like any other star in the sky. Although the Sun's light and heat never reach you, its gravity has you trapped.

For more than four billion years, you've been travelling slowly around the Sun, celebrating one birthday every 100,000 years. At least you're not alone. You are a part of a huge cloud of similar snowballs, although your nearest neighbour is millions of kilometres away. Still, you try not to complain.

Suddenly, an **asteroid** whooshes past, nudging you off course. You begin moving towards the Sun, travelling faster and faster the closer you get.

After a few thousand years, you are finally near enough to feel the Sun's heat. Your icy skin starts to melt. The escaping gas and dust surround you with a cloud larger than Jupiter and form a tail millions of kilometres long. Now you reflect so much sunlight you glow! But your moment in the Sun won't last long. Soon you'll be zooming back to the very edges of the solar system, for another few thousand years in the silent darkness.

Comets like this can appear from any direction. This has helped scientists to work out the size and shape of the Oort Cloud.

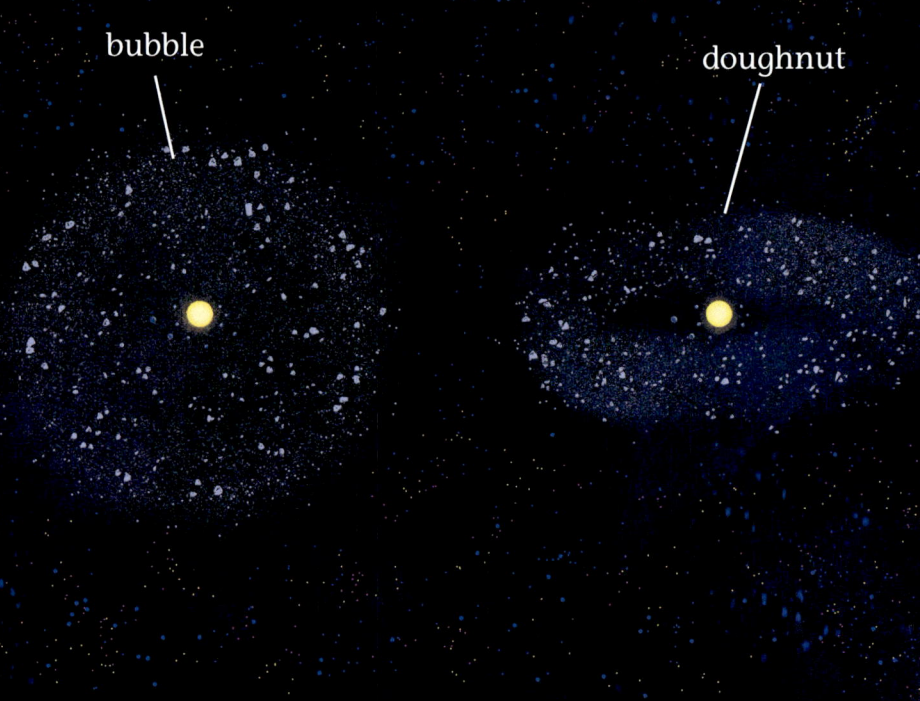

The Oort Cloud must be a giant bubble around the solar system. If it was shaped like a doughnut, comets would only come from a small ring of space, and not from other directions.

However, scientists still don't know exactly how big the Oort Cloud is.

Some think it starts around 2,000 times further from the Sun than Earth. Others say 5,000.

They also disagree on where it ends. Some think it might reach halfway from our Sun to the next nearest star!

Scientists always test their ideas!

Only one thing is certain: You'll need a lot of doughnuts for the journey!

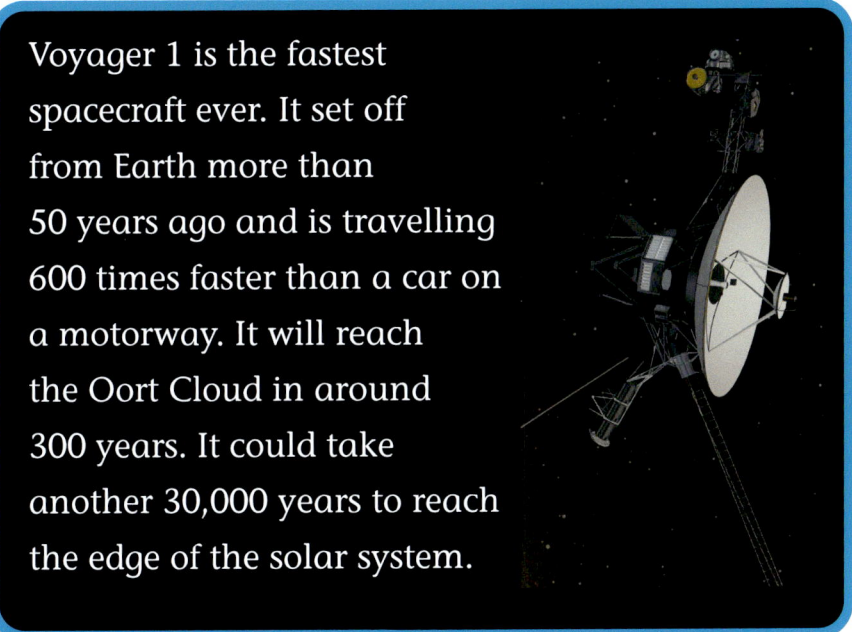

Voyager 1 is the fastest spacecraft ever. It set off from Earth more than 50 years ago and is travelling 600 times faster than a car on a motorway. It will reach the Oort Cloud in around 300 years. It could take another 30,000 years to reach the edge of the solar system.

3 We don't know ... how the planets got their strange features!

Scientists have photographed all sorts of solar system objects using powerful telescopes.

The James Webb Space Telescope is the largest and most powerful space telescope.

They have sent spacecraft to visit every planet, and many moons. They have landed on Venus, Mars and the Moon, and on comets and asteroids.

However, even the objects we know well have plenty of puzzles left to solve. Why are the planets so different from each other? How did they get their strange features? We cannot travel back in time and find answers.

We can only look for clues and try to piece together the past.

What toppled Uranus?

Uranus is a giant, icy planet in the outer solar system.

Most planets spin upright, like spinning tops. This is because they all formed from the same spinning disc of gas and dust, left over from when the Sun formed.

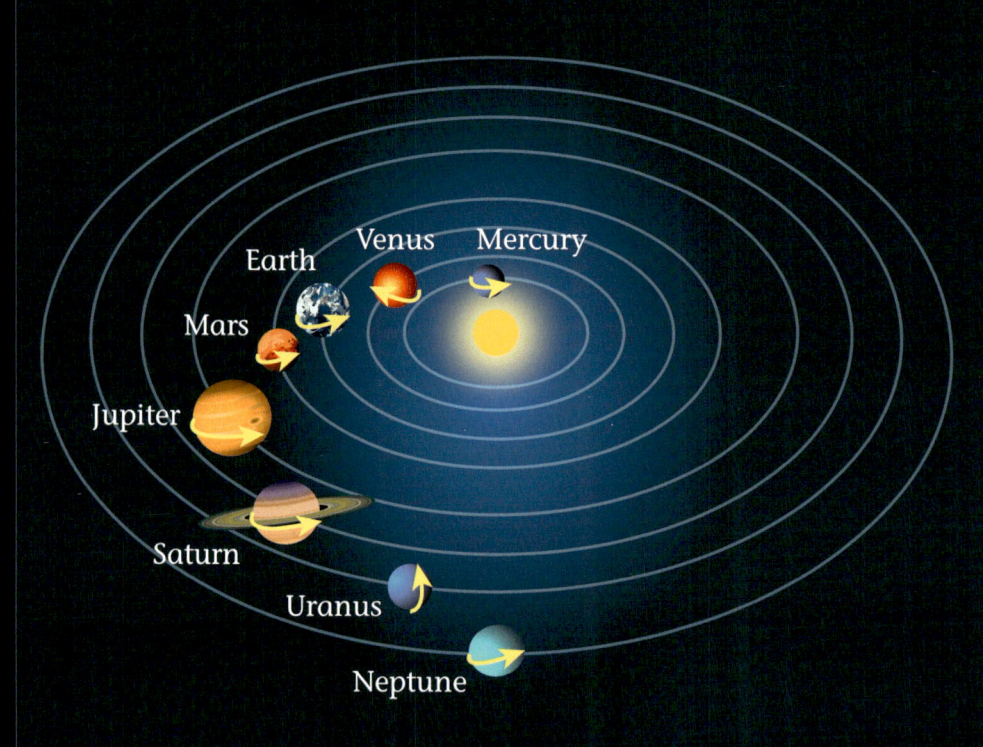

Uranus is the only planet to roll around the Sun on its side!

Because Uranus is tipped on its side, its rings seem to go from top to bottom.

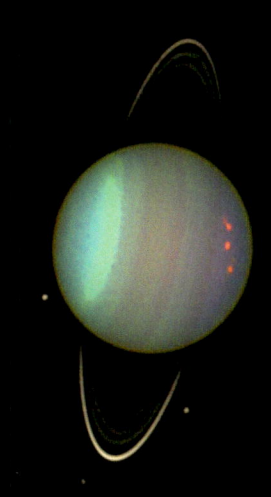

Scientists have come up with different ideas to explain this:

- 💡 It was knocked over in a giant crash with another planet.

- 💡 It began to wobble like a spinning top as it slows, ending up on its side.

- 💡 It was knocked over by lots of small **collisions**.

- 💡 It was pulled over by the gravity of a large moon, as it moved further away.

We'll never know for sure. Which idea do you think sounds most likely?

What lies beneath Venus's clouds?

Venus is one of the closest planets to Earth. It is surrounded by thick clouds. To find out what the surface looks like, scientists had to find a way to get under the clouds.

Several spacecraft have landed on Venus. But most were crushed and roasted in seconds!

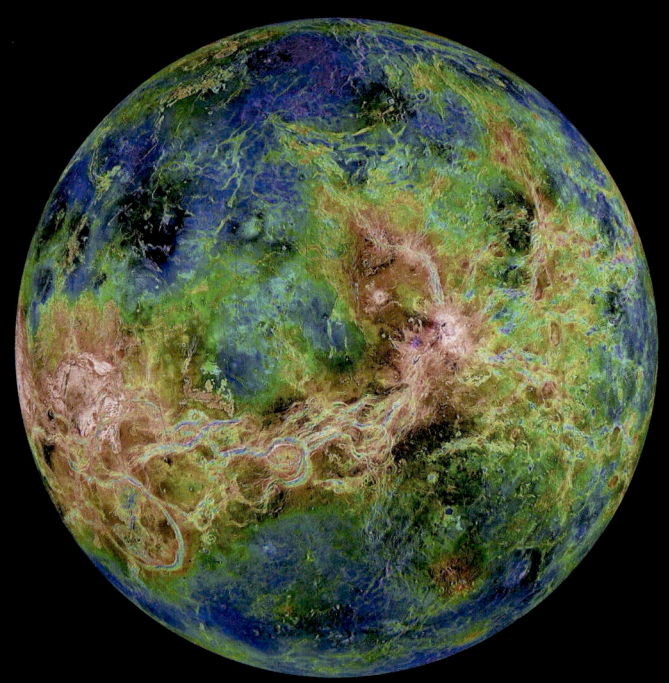

Venus is the hottest planet in the solar system.
The surface is hot enough to cook a pizza in seconds.

Only four landers survived long enough to send back pictures of Venus's surface.

These pictures were taken in 1975 and 1982.

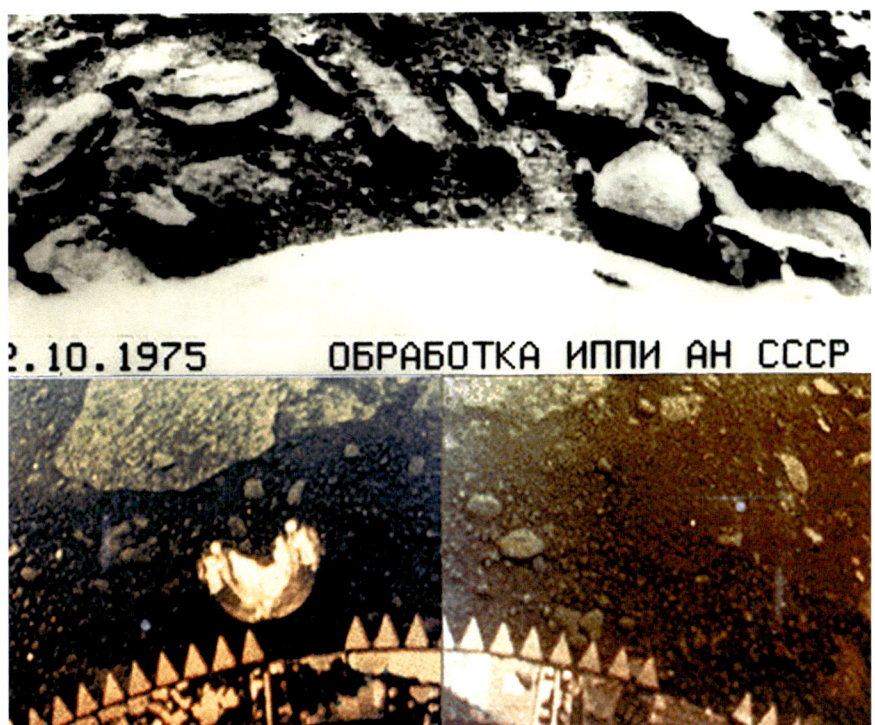

Scientists want to go back to Venus to find out more. Venus has 85,000 volcanoes. Today it is a hot and dry place, but scientists have spotted a little water in its thick clouds. They think it once had a watery ocean. It may even have had living things!

Why are there blueberries on Mars?

Robotic rovers have driven across Mars's rocky red surface. They have taken photos, scooped soil and drilled into rocks. They have also looked for fossils and other signs of **ancient** life.

Along the way, the rovers have spotted some very strange things. Could they be signs of life?

Opportunity rover spotted these 'blueberries' in a crater on Mars. They might have been formed by **microbes** that lived millions of years ago. They do prove that Mars was once covered in water, because similar ball-shaped rocks have formed in watery places on Earth.

The 'leopard spots' on this rock could have been left behind by tiny living things. Or they could have been formed in a volcano.

The Curiosity rover found a rock that looks just like coral. However, scientists think it is more likely to be a rock that formed when the planet was wet.

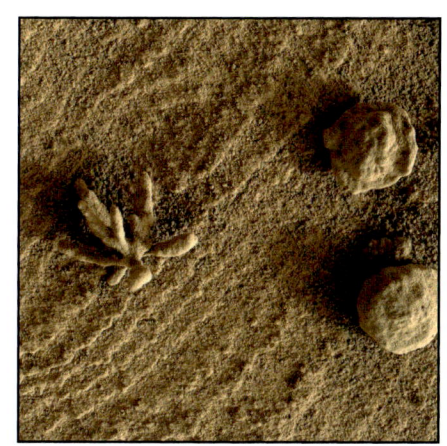

Today's Mars rovers can only send back pictures and sounds. In the future, scientists hope to return rocks and soil from Mars to Earth.

Why are Saturn's moons so strange?

Saturn has at least 274 moons. That's more than any other planet in our solar system!

Each one is very different from the others. The largest is Titan, a moon larger than the planet Mercury!
It even has rivers and lakes on its surface. The smallest is just a large, dry **boulder**.

In between, there are many moons with puzzling features.

Hyperion has craters so deep it looks like a sponge. So why doesn't it collapse?

Enceladus has an underground ocean. But why is some of the salty water spraying out into space?

Why are the tiny moons Pan and Atlas shaped like flying saucers? Could they have formed from smaller moonlets that got stuck together?

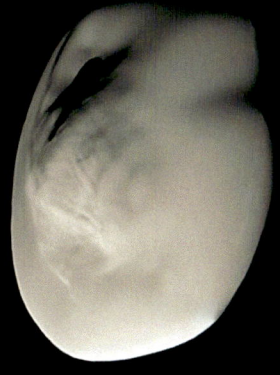 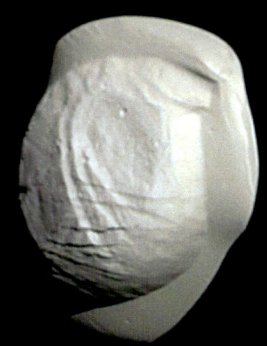

What makes egg-shaped Methone so smooth, without a single hill or crater? Could it be covered in 'snow' from Saturn's icy rings?

Phoebe is much darker than most of Saturn's other moons. It is made of very different material from the other moons, too. Is it a comet captured by Saturn's gravity?

How did Earth's moon get here?

Earth may only have one moon, but it has plenty of puzzles to solve.

The biggest mystery is how the Moon formed in the first place.

Scientists have come up with different ideas. Which do you think sounds most likely?

1 A chunk of Earth broke off.

2 The Moon formed somewhere else. It drifted too close to Earth and was captured by our planet's gravity.

3 The Earth and Moon formed at the same time.

4 An asteroid crashed into Earth, throwing a huge amount of rubble into space. The Moon formed from this rubble.

At the moment, most scientists think idea number 4 is correct. But this could change as they collect more evidence.

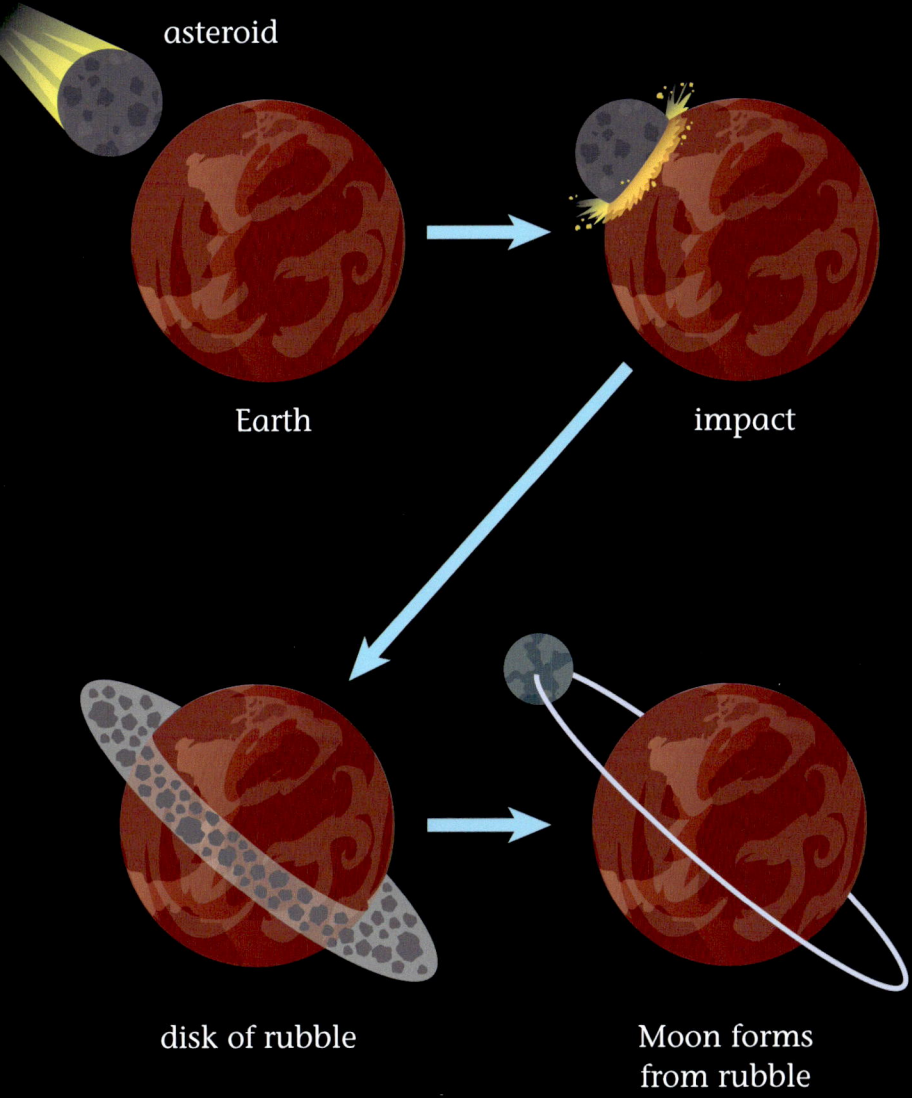

4 We don't know ... how the Sun works!

The Sun is a star, like the other stars you can see in the night sky.

However, the Sun is much closer to Earth than these other stars. It is so close that it lights and heats our planet. Without the Sun, Earth would be dark and frozen.

Thanks to the Sun, scientists have found out a lot about stars. All stars are fiery balls of hot gas. Some of their light and heat escapes and zooms out across space.

However, there are still lots of questions left to answer.

Plants use the Sun's energy to grow. Animals eat plants to get this energy. All the energy in your food began as sunlight!

Why is the space around the Sun much hotter than its surface?

The area of space around the Sun is called the corona.

corona

Strangely, the corona becomes hotter the further away you get from the Sun's surface. In some places, the corona is 350 times hotter than the surface.

This is like a bonfire feeling hotter as you walk away from it!

The heat comes from the Sun itself. But why does so much of it hang around in the corona, instead of escaping into outer space?

To help solve this mystery, scientists sent two spacecraft to investigate.

Parker Solar Probe was the first spacecraft ever to enter the corona and touch the Sun.

A foam shield protects Parker Solar Probe from the scorching heat.

Can we predict explosions on the Sun's surface?

From Earth, the Sun seems to burn steadily. Up close, it's a different story.

Warning!
Never look directly at the Sun, even when wearing dark glasses.

Around once a week, there is a huge eruption on the Sun's surface. Huge clouds of plasma are blasted into space.

A few days later, the clouds slam into Earth's atmosphere. They cause solar storms.

Solar storms cause the Northern and Southern Lights, but they can also damage **satellites** and cause power cuts. Every year the damage costs a huge amount of money to fix.

The pretty colours of the Northern Lights are caused by particles from the Sun crashing into Earth's air.

Solar storms are dangerous for living things too. They can cause animals such as whales to lose their way and get stuck in the wrong place.

Every 11 years, the Sun becomes extra fiery. Eruptions happen two or three times every day. This means more and bigger solar storms. Scientists would like to understand why this happens. They would like to find ways to predict solar storms.

What does the Sun look like inside?

We know a lot about the Sun's surface. This is the only part of the Sun we can see.

Scientists believe they have worked out what the Sun (and other stars) might look like inside.

Convective Zone

Radiative Zone

Core

The **core** is where the Sun burns its fuel, releasing energy.

 15 million °C

If we could cut the Sun open like an orange, this is what it might look like. The good news is, there are no pips!

The energy slowly escapes to the surface.
This can take a million years.

2 million °C

Chromosphere

Photosphere

At the surface, the heat escapes into space.

5,500 °C

One day, scientists hope to invent tools that can peer through the hot, bright surface to see if these ideas are right.

Space detectives

We know lots about our solar system, but there is even more that we don't know!

How did Earth's moon form?

Does our solar system have a ninth planet?

Do any surprises lurk beneath Venus's clouds?

Are there any signs of life on Mars?

Do comets really come from the Oort Cloud?

What does the Sun look like inside?

How big is the solar system?

If you become a space scientist, you could help to answer some of these questions!

Which ones would you most like to solve?

Glossary

ancient	very old
asteroid	a small lump of dusty rock that orbits the Sun
black hole	the squashed-together remains of an old star, with very strong gravity
boulder	a large lump of rock that is not attached to anything
collisions	crashes between two objects
comets	frozen lumps of ice or rubble, orbiting the Sun
core	the very centre of something
dwarf planet	a spherical object in space that looks like a small planet
evidence	facts or information that support an idea
gravity	the force that pulls objects towards each other; larger objects have stronger gravity
microbes	the smallest living things, too small to be seen without a microscope
orbits	the path that one object in space takes around another

satellites   small objects that orbit bigger objects in space

solar system   the Sun and everything that orbits it

telescopes   tools to make far-away objects look bigger and brighter, so we can see them

Index

comets 16–20

Mars 4, 23, 28–29

moons 5, 9, 30–31, 32–33

Northern Lights 38–39

Oort Cloud 15–17, 20–21

Planet Nine 6–11

Pluto 4–5, 8–9

Saturn 4–5, 30–31

Sedna 14

Sun 2–3, 5, 6, 9, 12, 34–41

Uranus 4–5, 9, 24–25

Venus 4, 23, 26–27

An astronaut's diary

I am standing on a giant object, smaller than Earth but larger than the planet Mercury. The Sun is so far away it looks 10 times smaller than it does from Earth. However, its dim light is reflected by sparkling rings around a nearby planet.

Around me, I can see other moons with all kinds of shapes and textures. I'm sure an egg just floated past! The object I'm standing on is also icy, but there is liquid here too. It has rivers, lakes and seas, but they are not made from water.

Where am I?

Ideas for reading

Written by Gill Matthews
Primary Literacy Consultant

Reading objectives:
- be introduced to non-fiction books that are structured in different ways
- draw on what they already know or on background information and vocabulary provided by the teacher
- explain and discuss their understanding of books, poems and other material, both those that they listen to and those that they read for themselves

Spoken language objectives:
- participate in discussion
- speculate, hypothesise, imagine and explore ideas through talk

Curriculum links: Science: Living things and their habitats

Word count: 3149

Interest words: senses, clear, still, empty

Resources: ICT for research, paper and pens

Build a context for reading

- Ask children to look at the front cover of the book and to read the title.
- Discuss what the title means to them.
- Read the back cover blurb.
- Explore what they know about space and the planets. Discuss what Planet Nine might be.
- Point out that this is an information book. Ask what features they expect to find in the book. Give children a few minutes to skim through the book, looking for the features they identified.

Understand and apply reading strategies

- Read pp2–3 aloud. Ask children what they think they are going to find out from the book.